BERMUDA
Sketch Coloring Book

BEST IN TRAVEL 2017

-

TOP 10 COUNTRIES YOU DO NOT MISS IN 2017
(Volume 5)

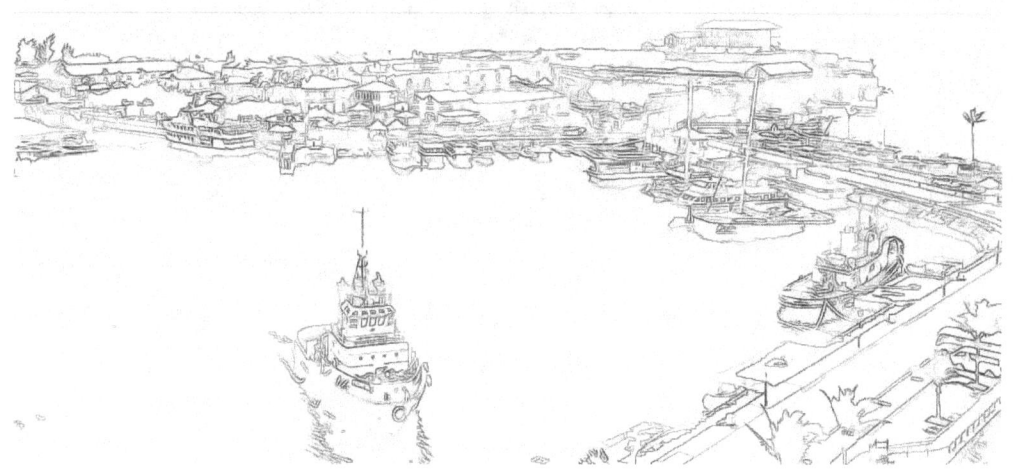

Anthony Hutzler

Sketch Coloring Book

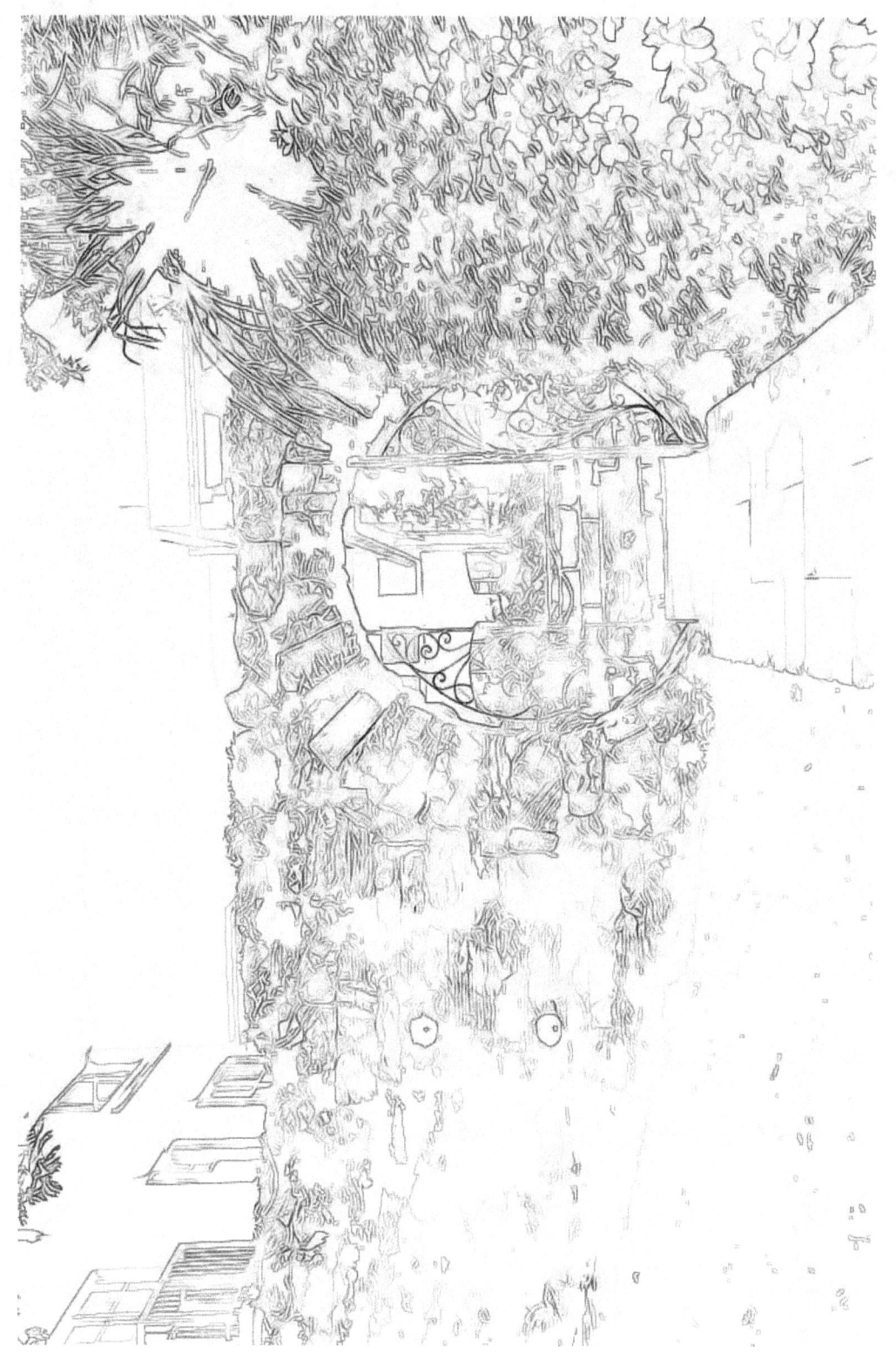

An old stone wall with a moon gate in Queens Park, Hamilton Bermuda

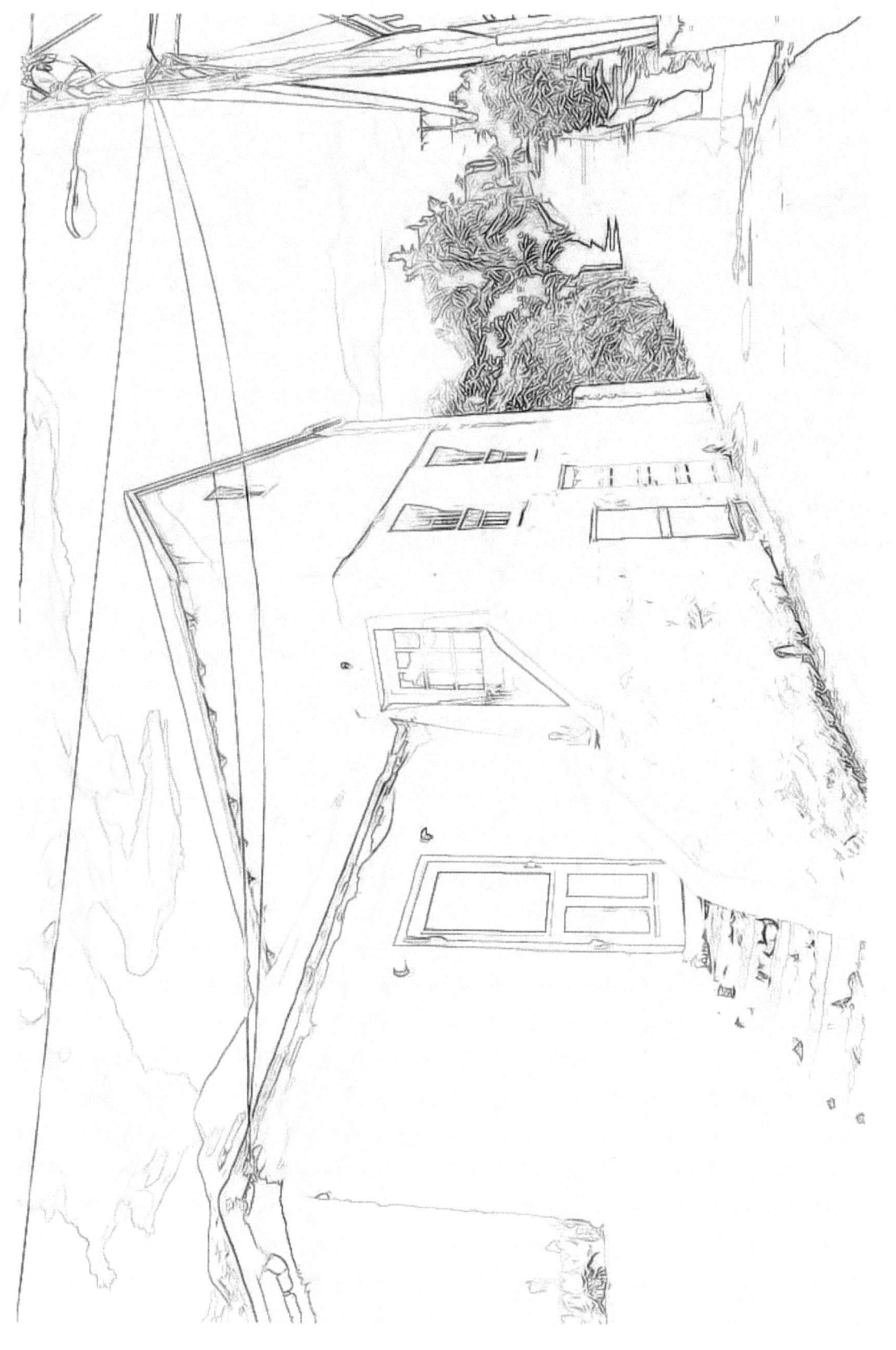

A rustic white home along a rural road on May 27 2016 in St. Georgea's Bermuda

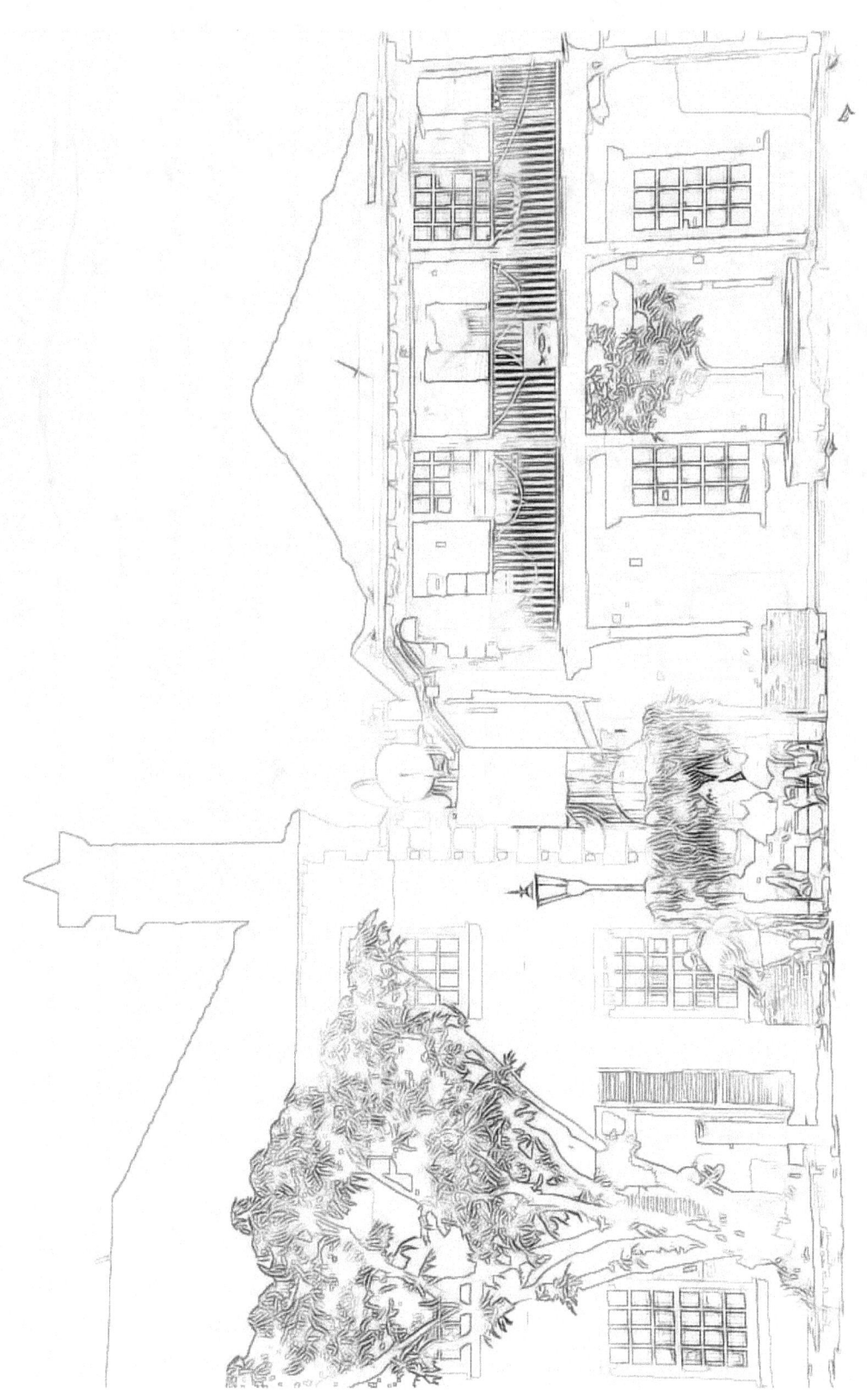

Colorful buildings with white roofs to collect water on May 27 2016 in St. George's Bermuda.

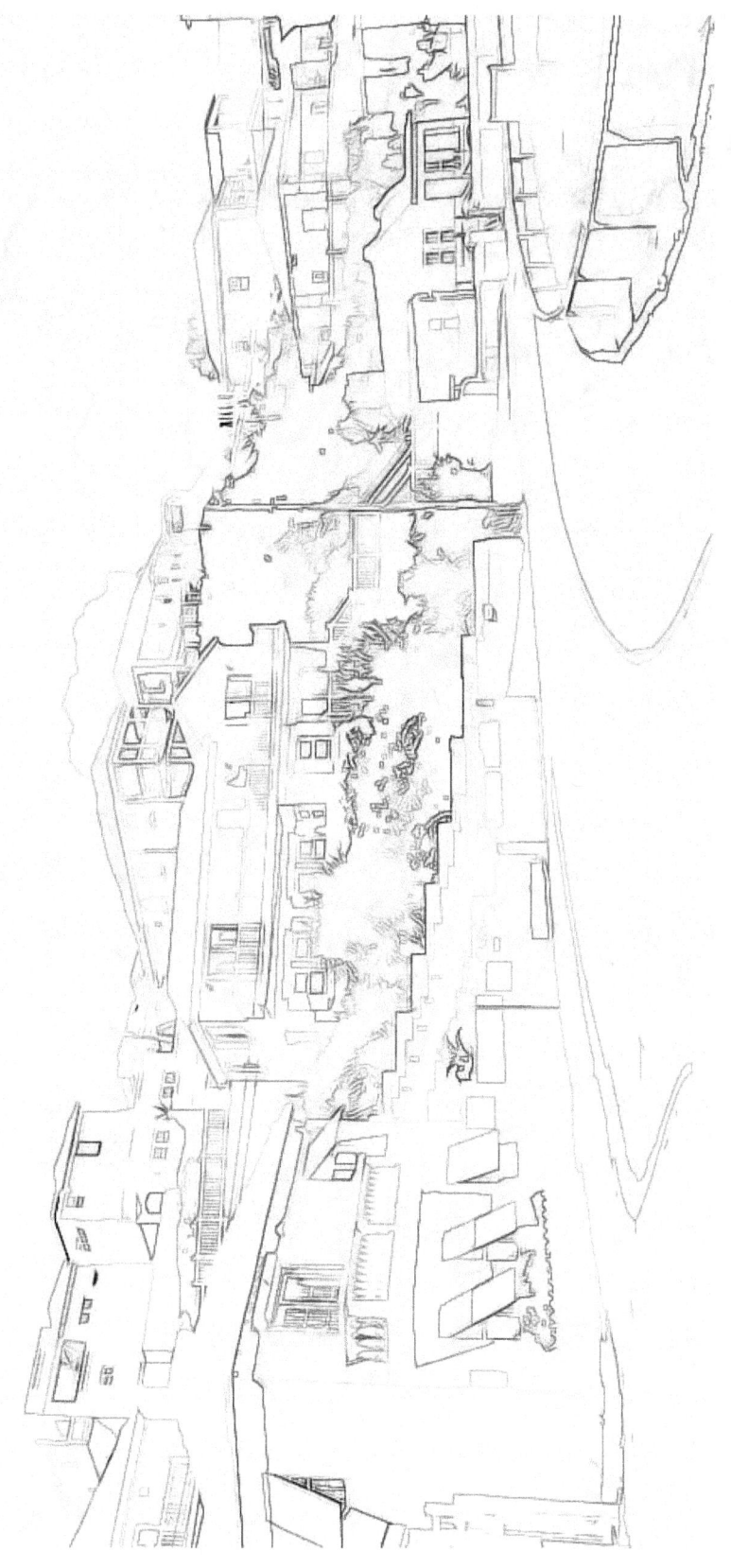

Tropical Colors

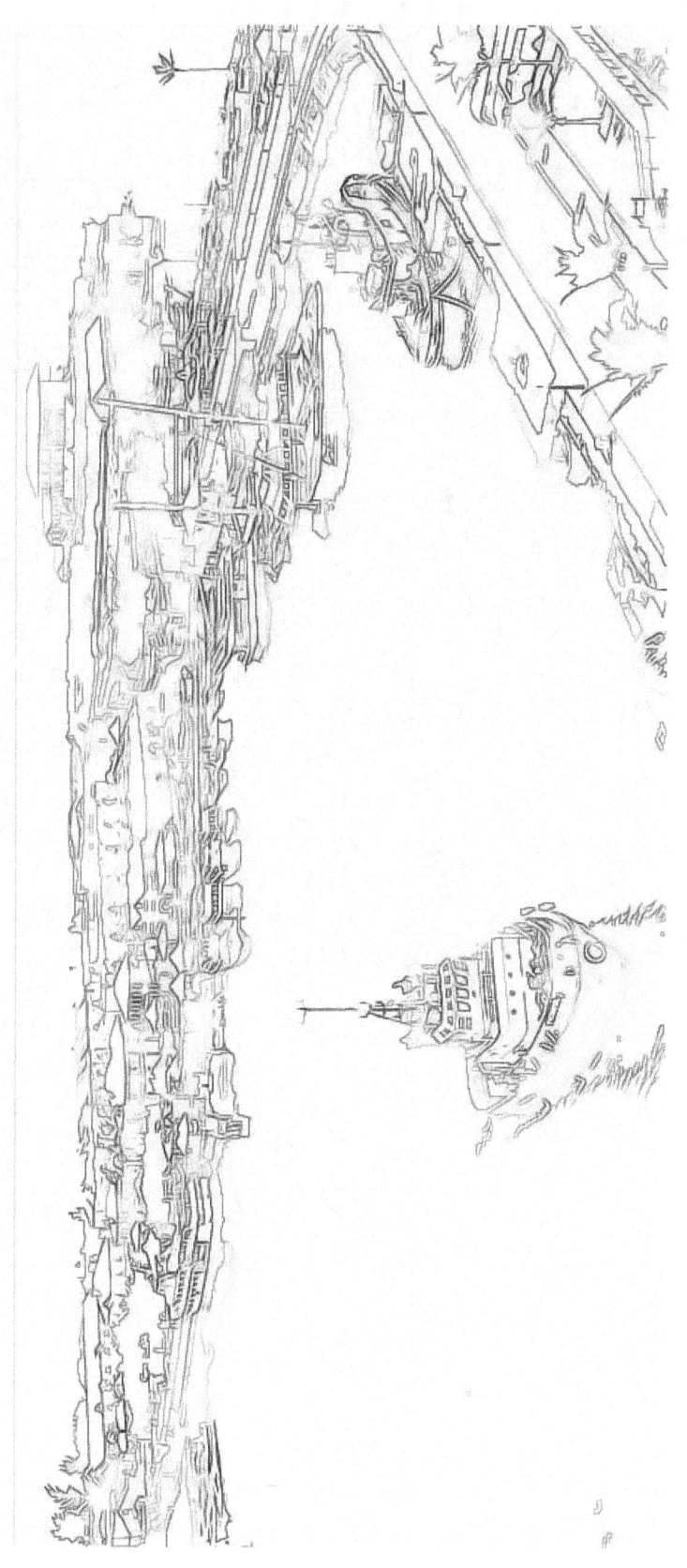

A scenic view of the Royal Naval Dockyard on May 25 2016 in Bermuda.

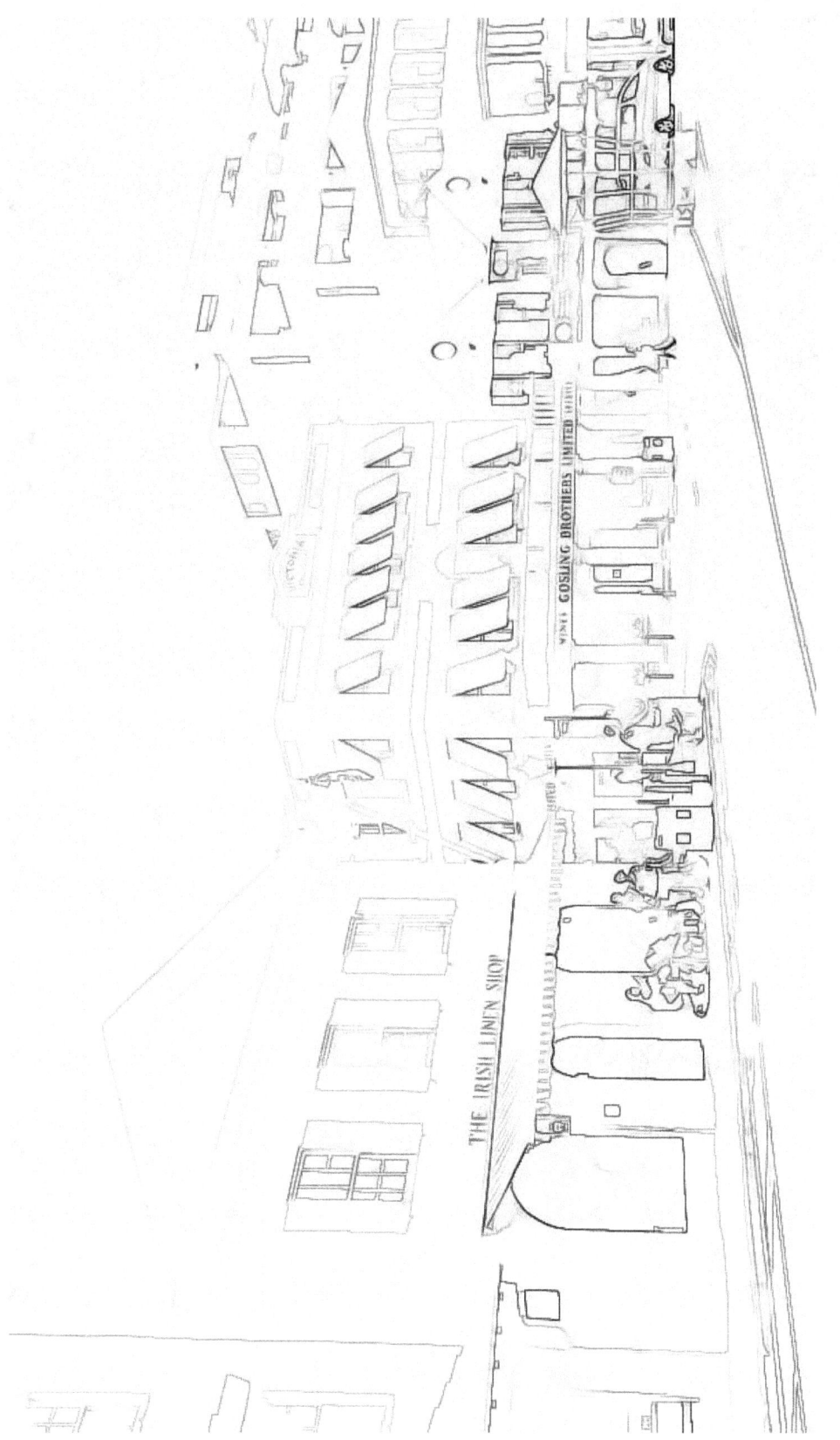

A colorful downtown section across from the ferry terminal on May 25 2016 in Hamilton,Bermuda

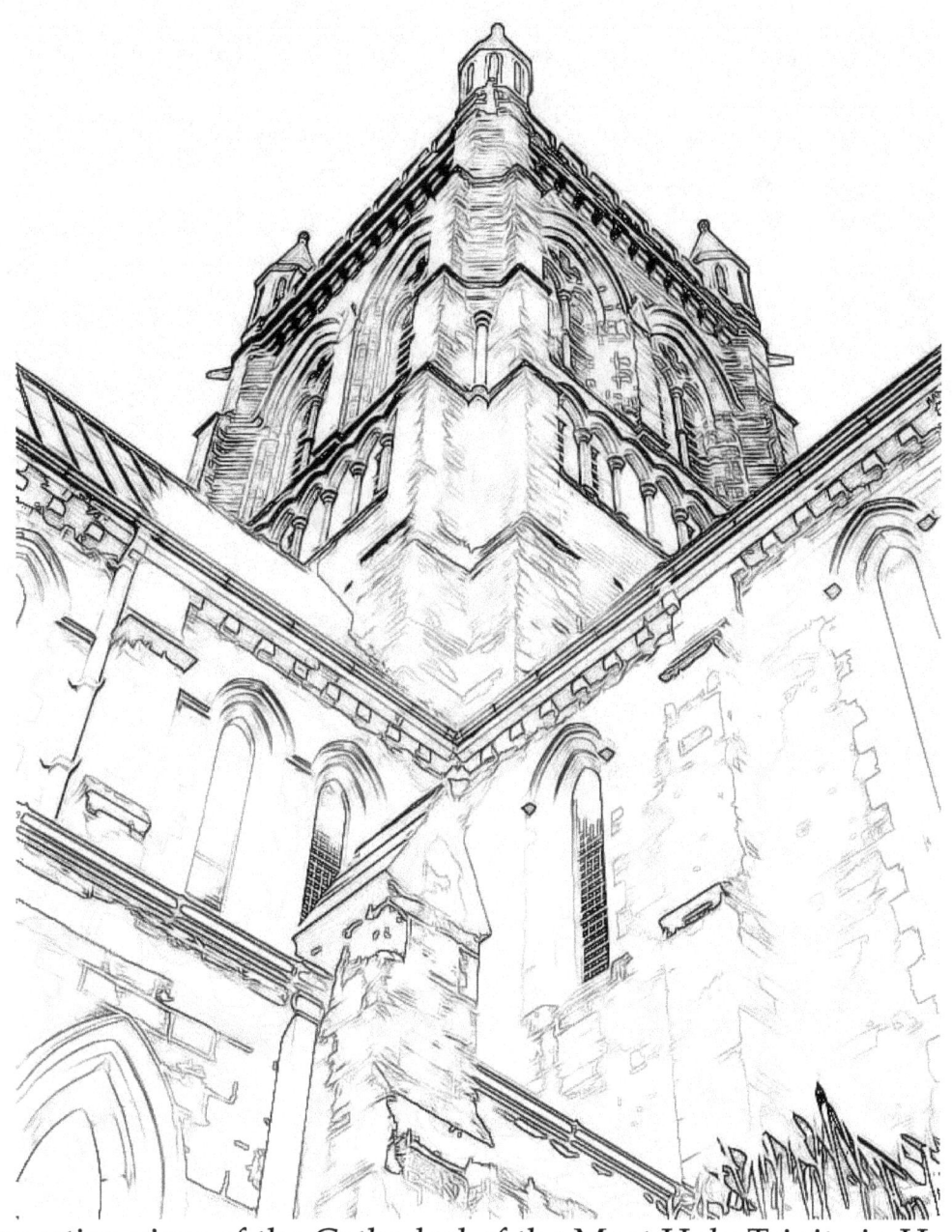

A perspective view of the Cathedral of the Most Holy Trinity in Hamilton Bermuda.

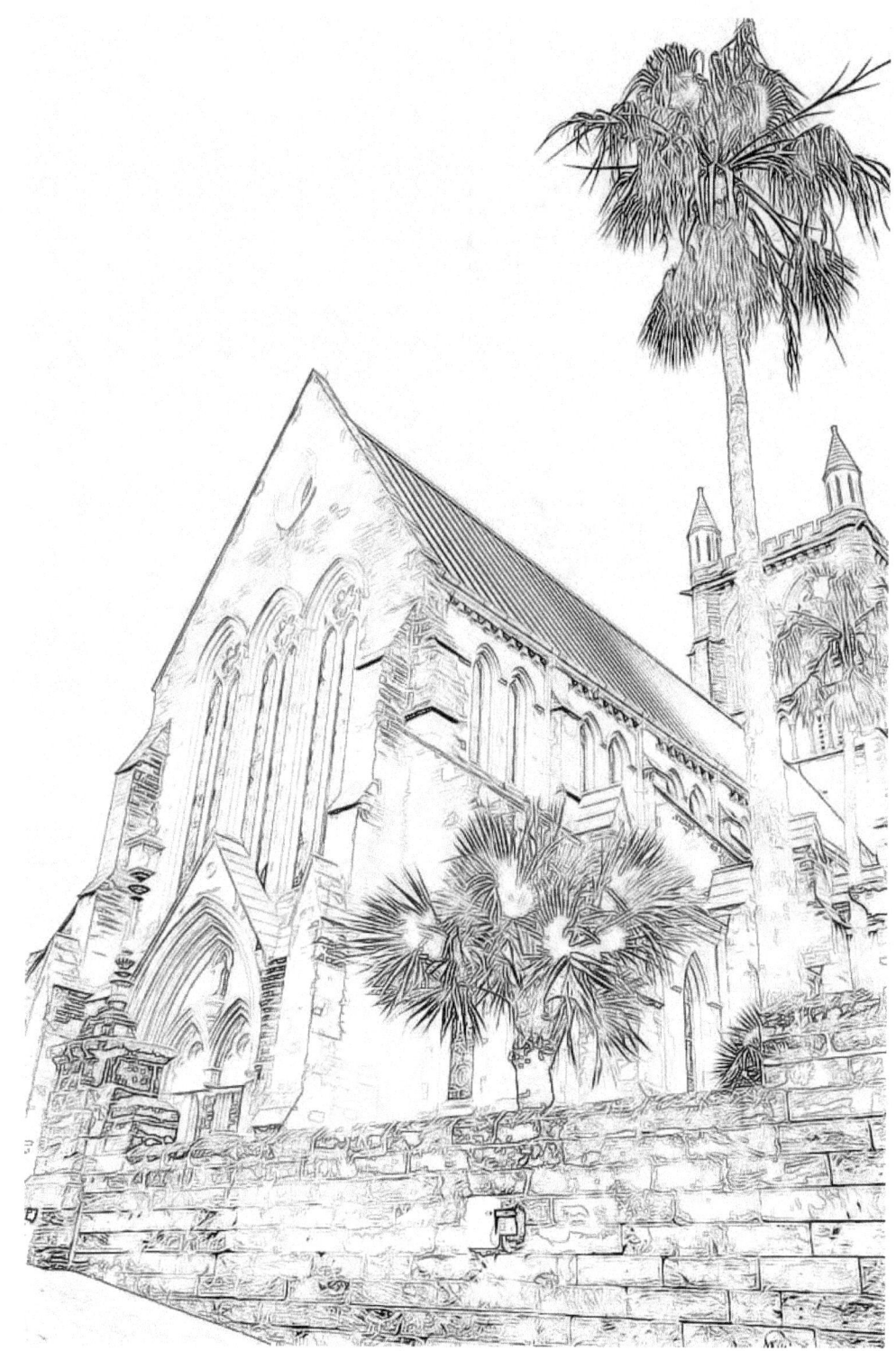

The Cathedral of the Most Holy Trinity a historic Anglican church in Hamilton Bermuda.

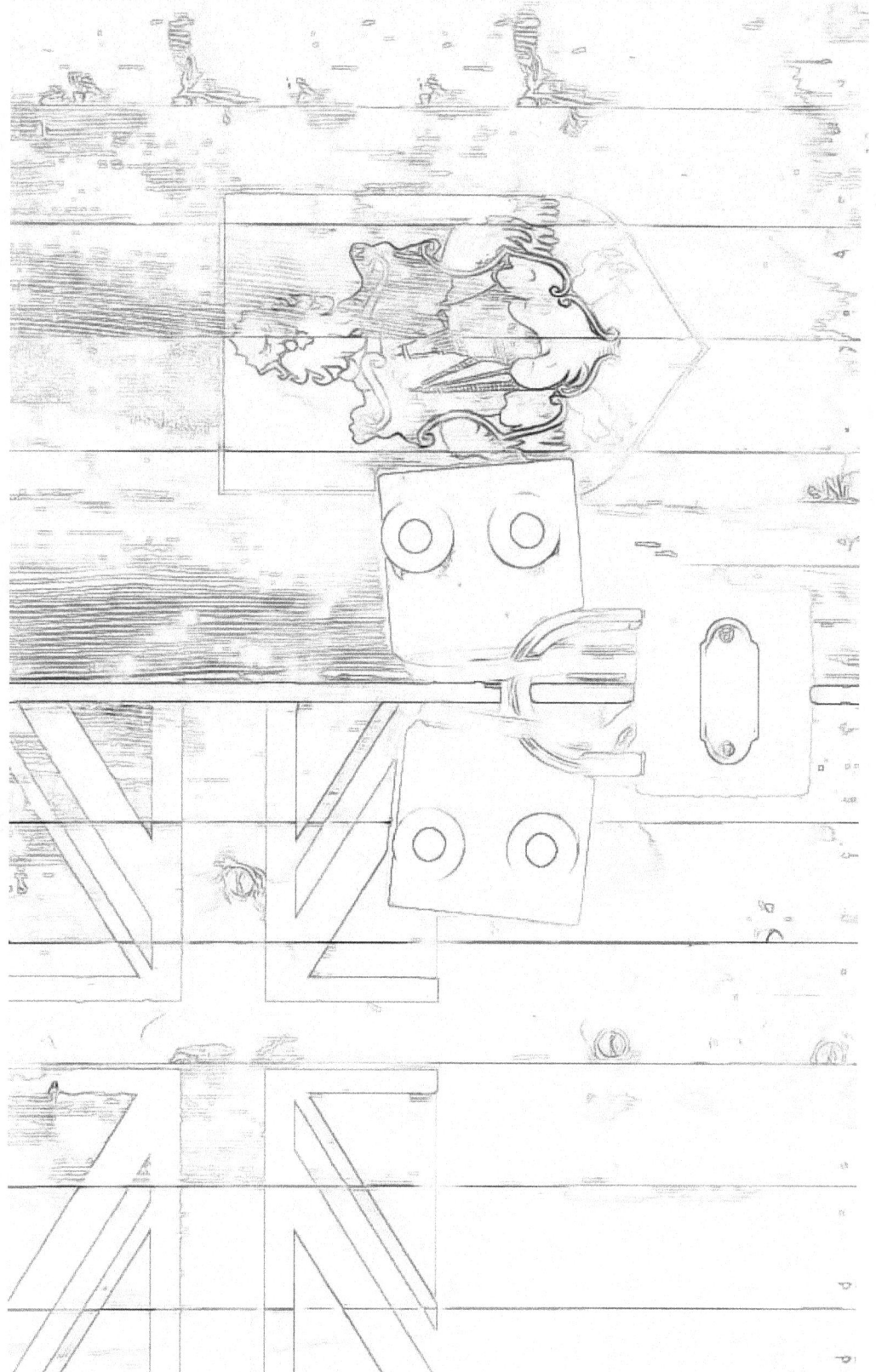

Bermuda flag on door with padlock

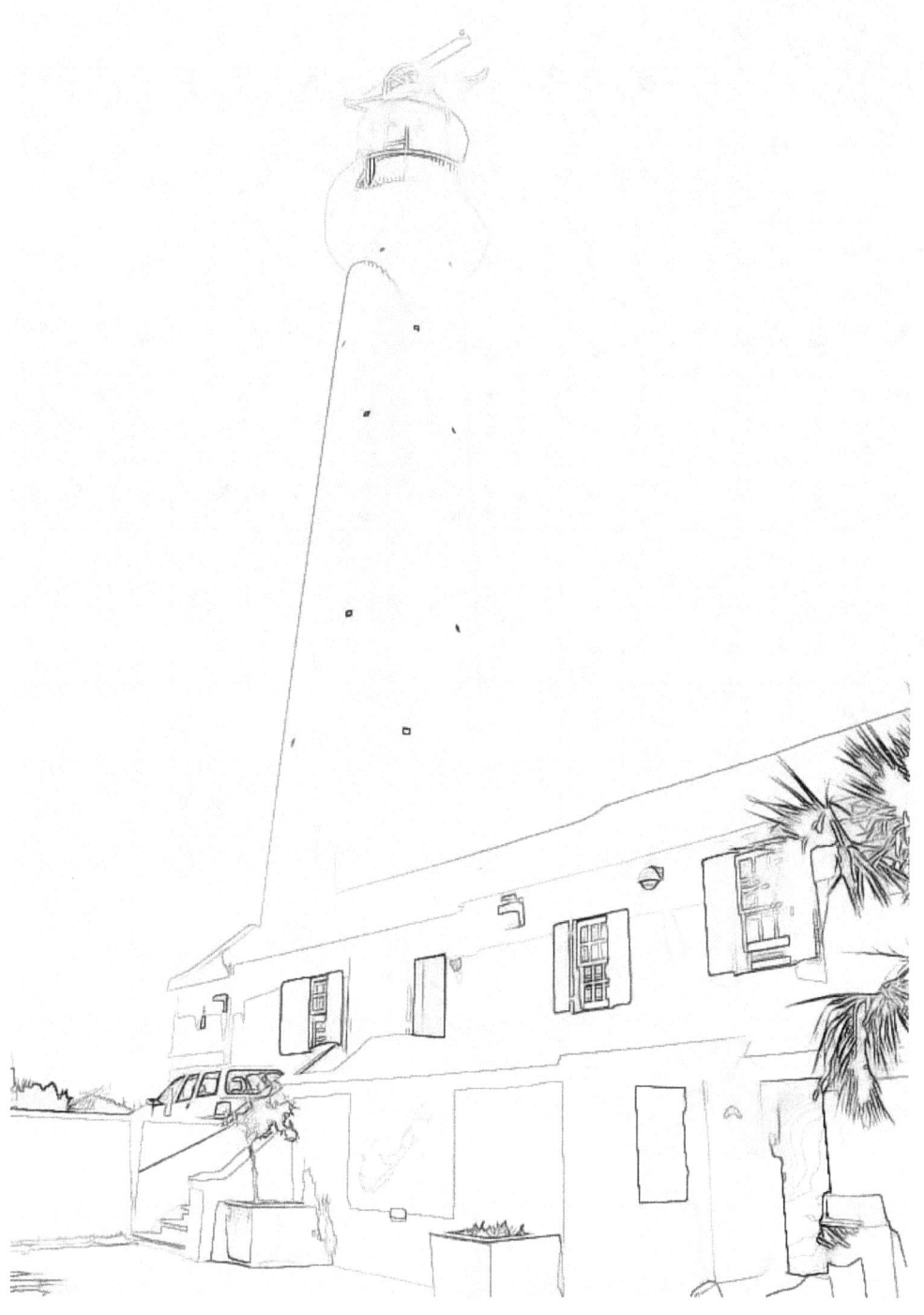

Gibbs Hill Lighthouse in Bermuda

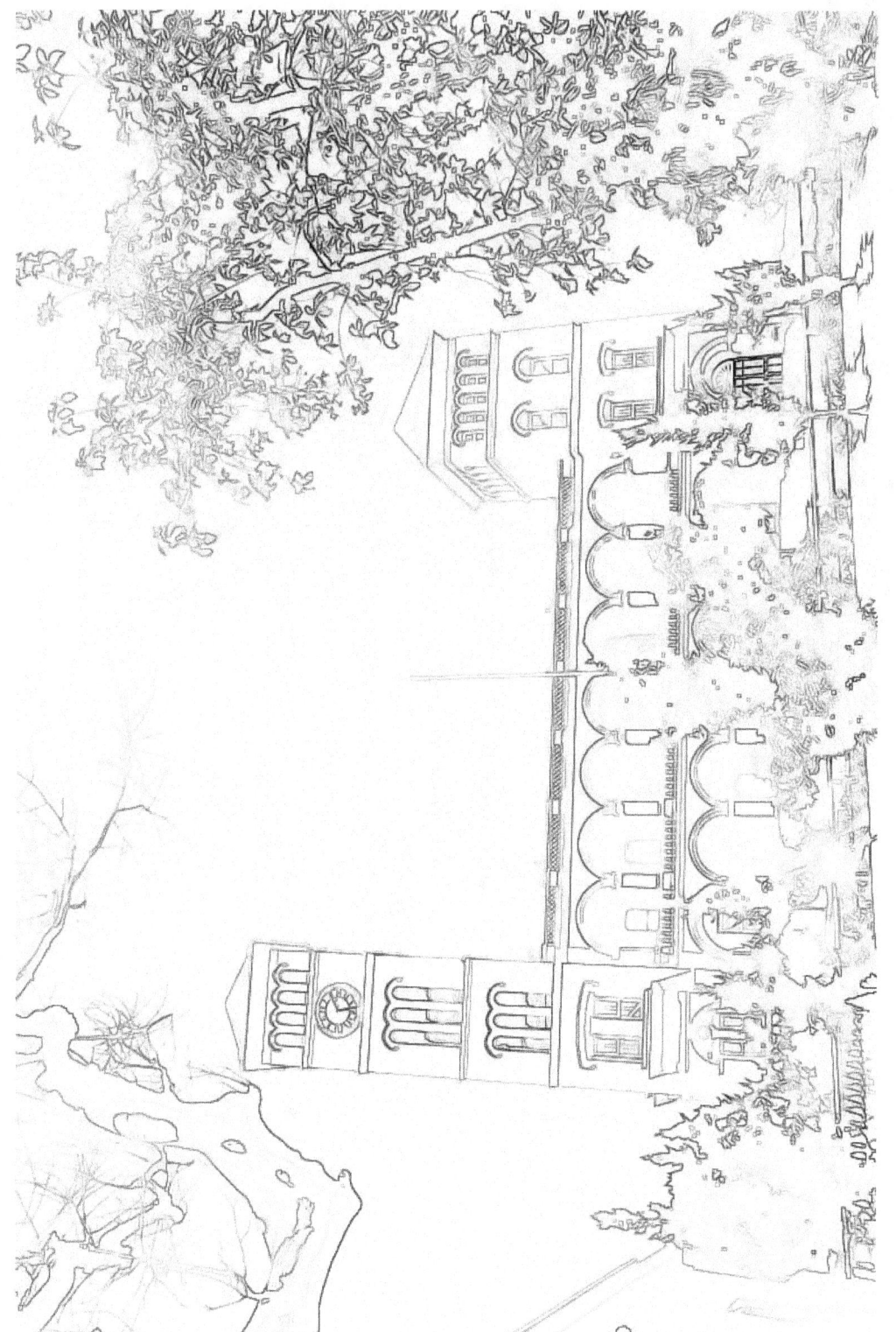

Sessions House on Parliament Hill, Bermuda

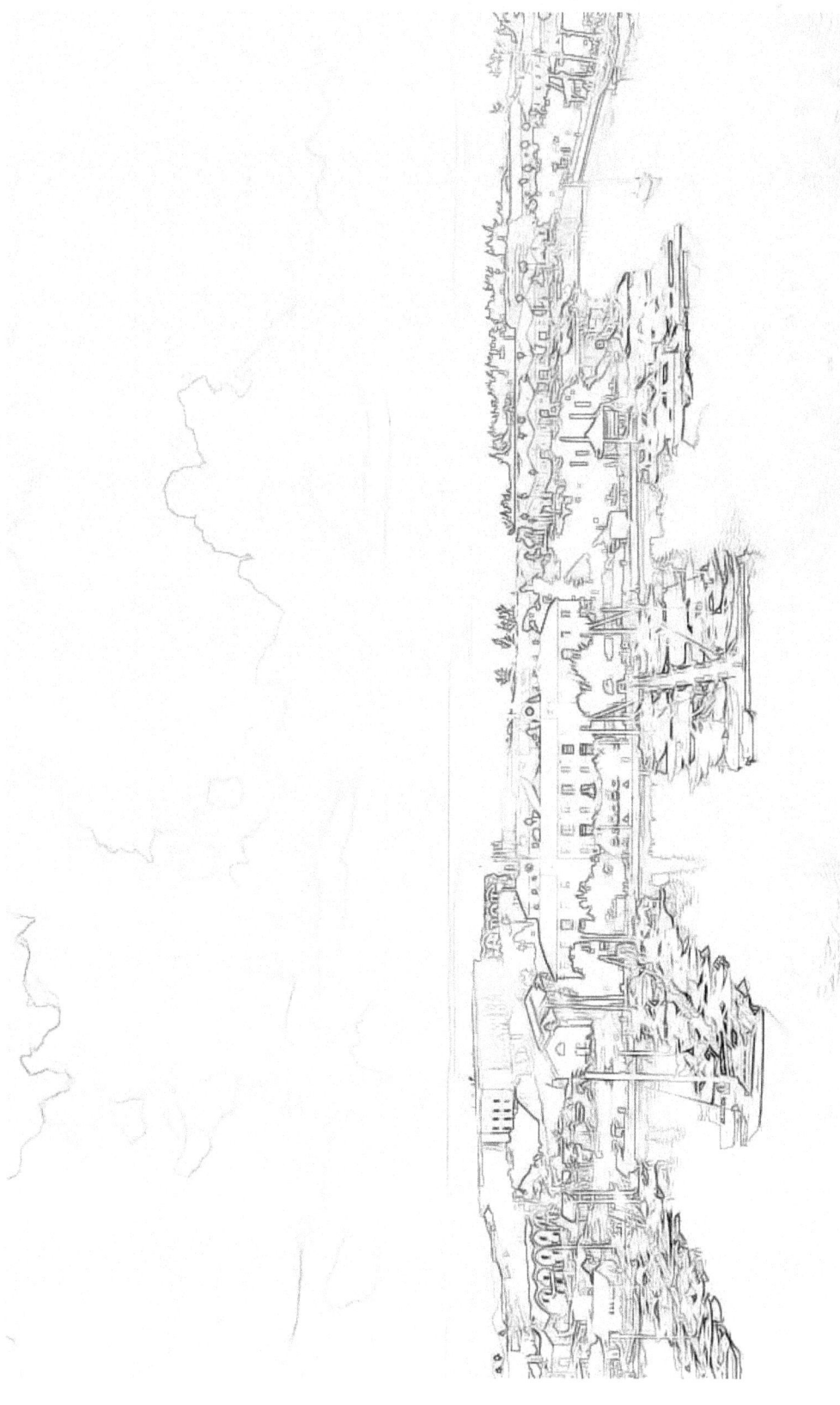

port in bermuda island with docked boats

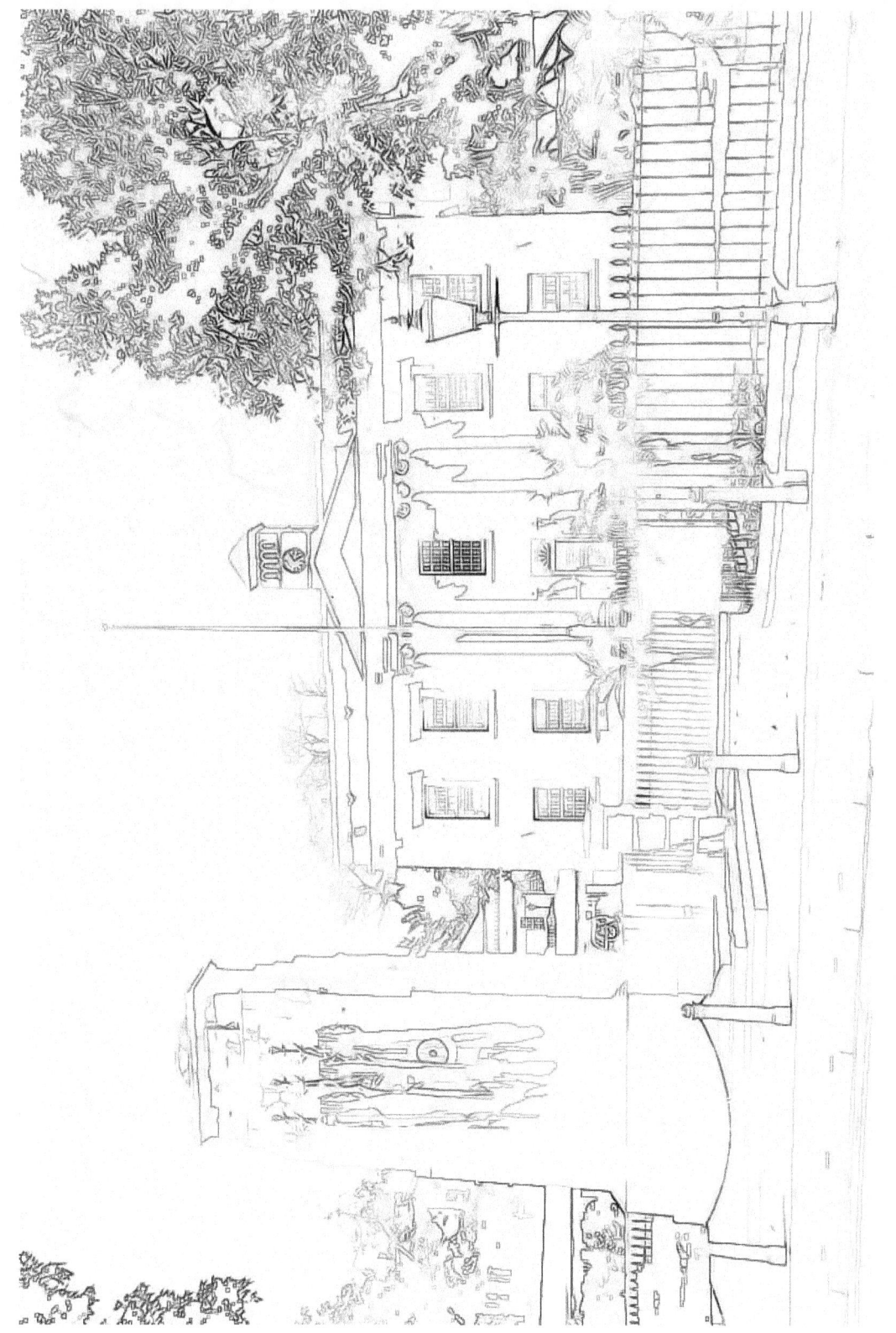

Senate of Bermuda or Cabinet Office, part of the parliment of Bermuda in Hamilton

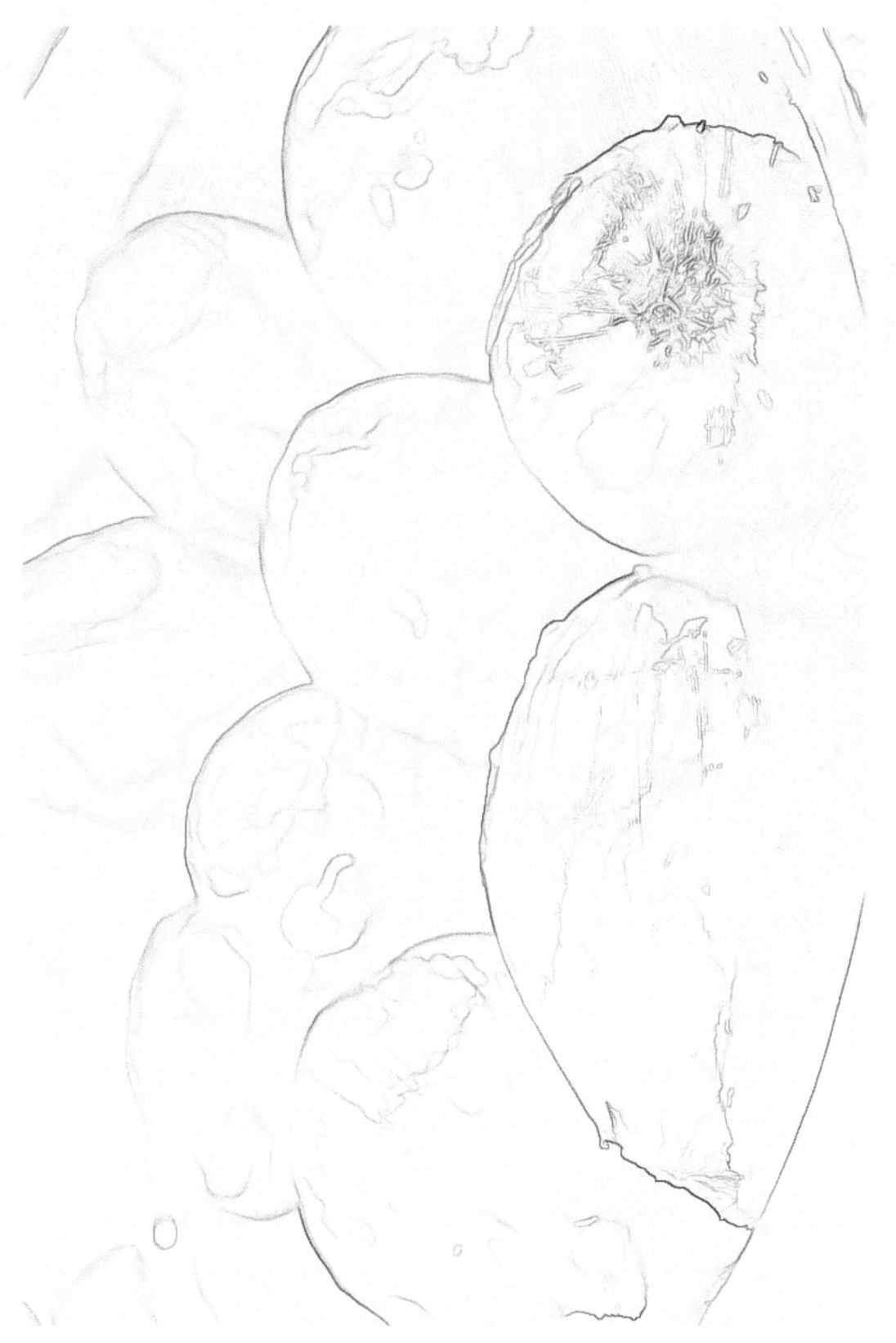

Whole red onions, sometimes called Bombay or Bermuda onions

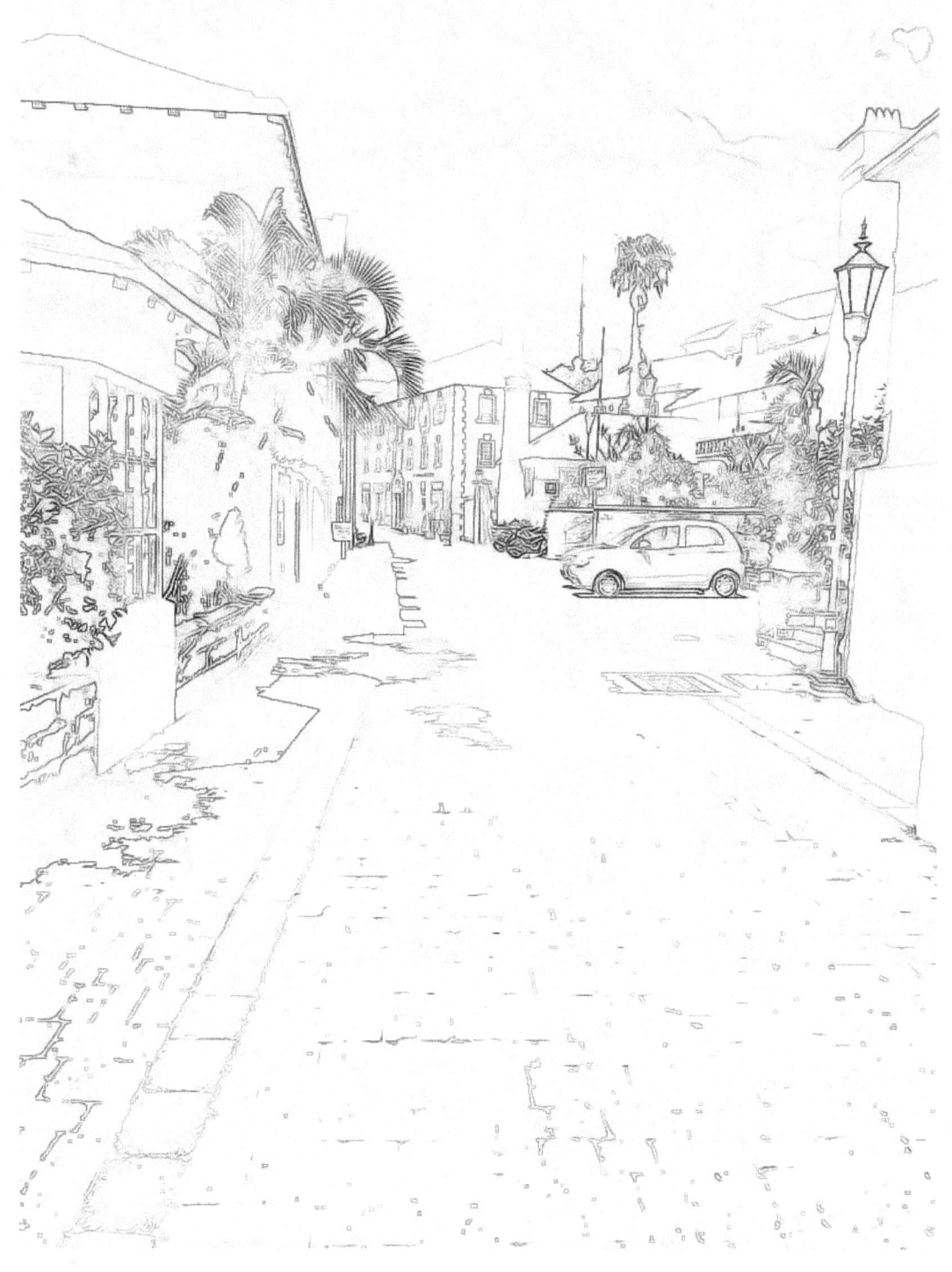

Colorful style architecture and white roof shops of St. George

Chappel

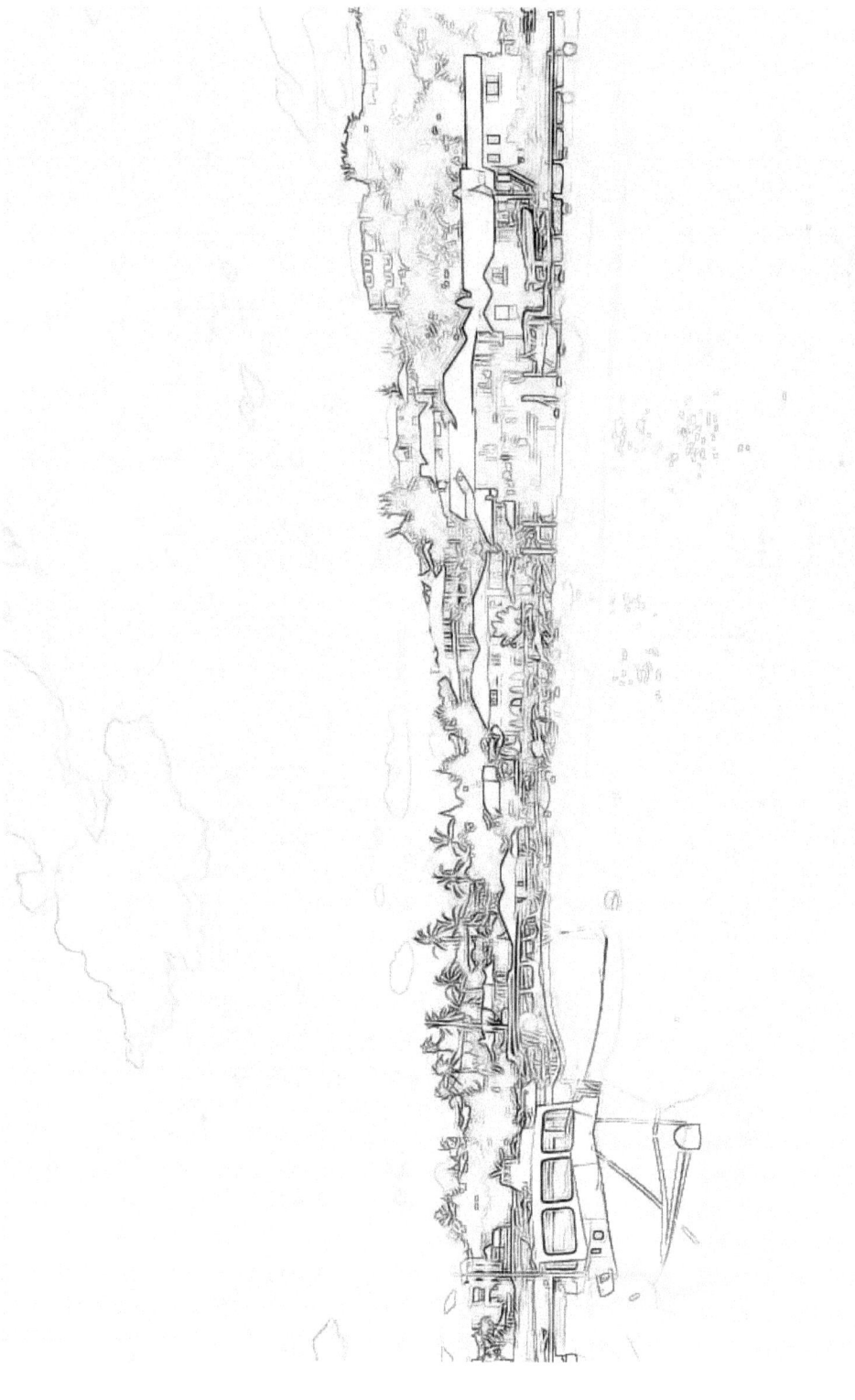

tropical bay or harbor beach of turquoise sea with modern yachts
marine boats vessels at moorage on sunny day on blue sky

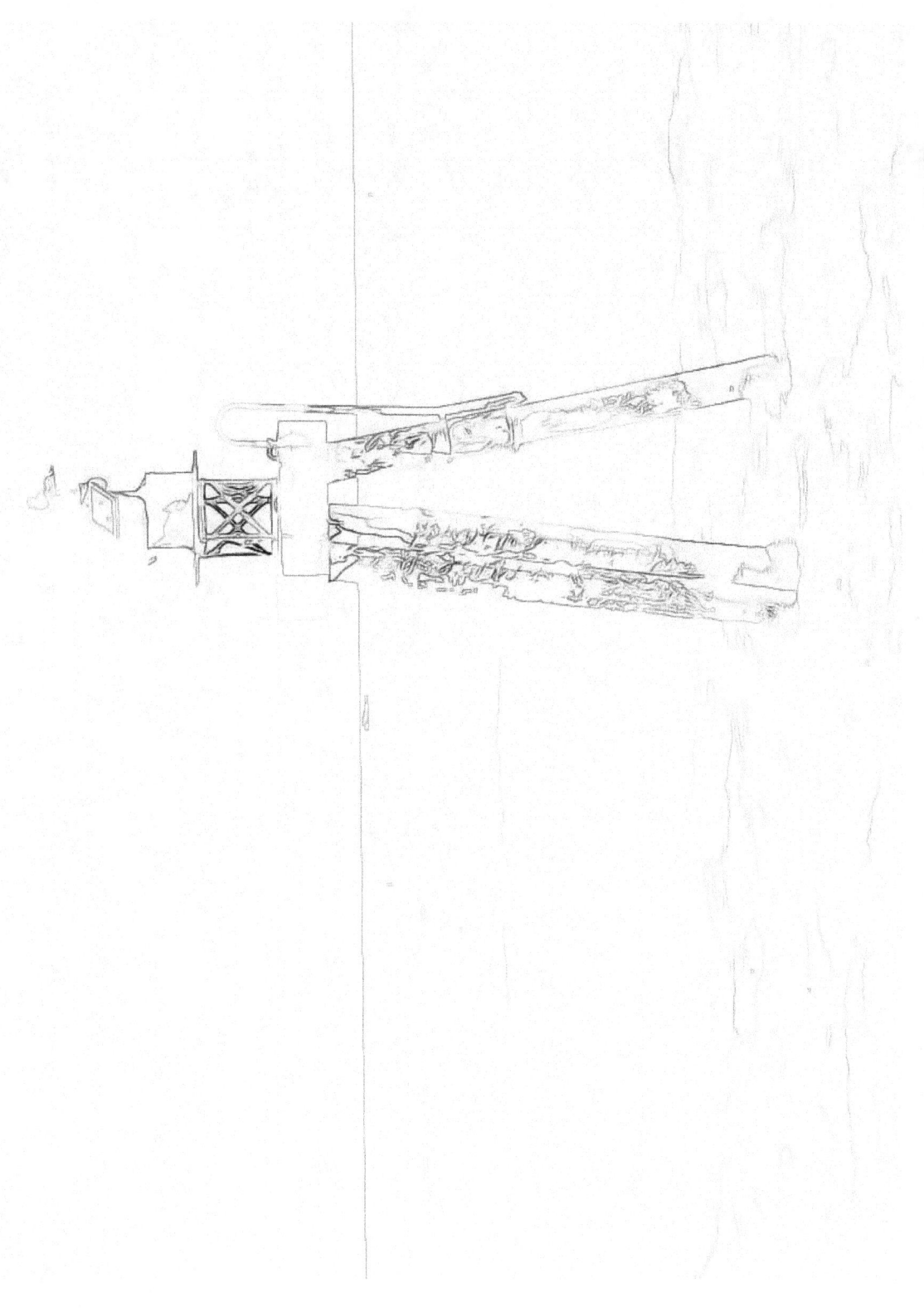

Navigation light in the Caribbean sea with a Seagull resting on the top

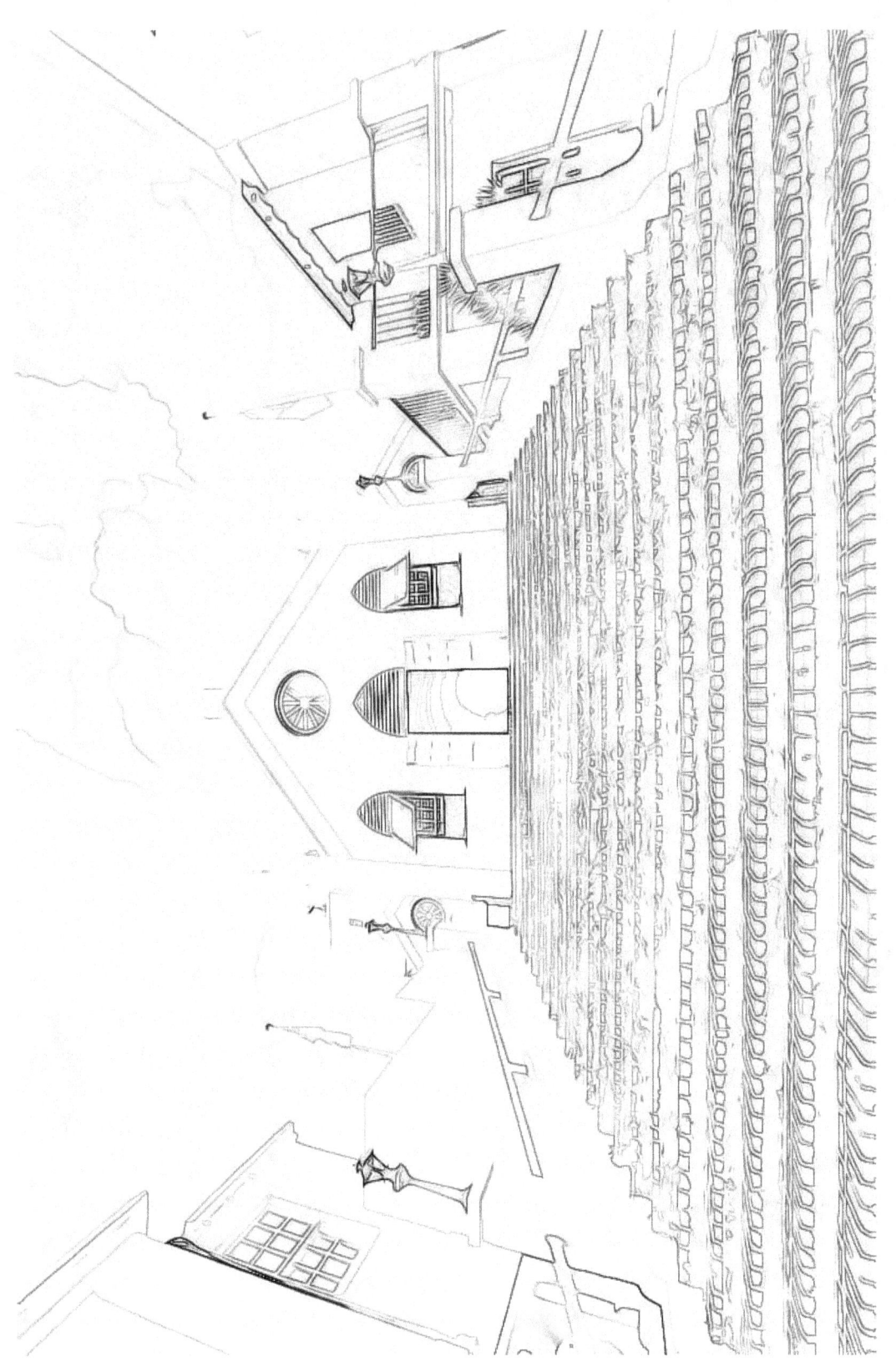

Bermuda Bermuda's oldest church St. Peters in St. George

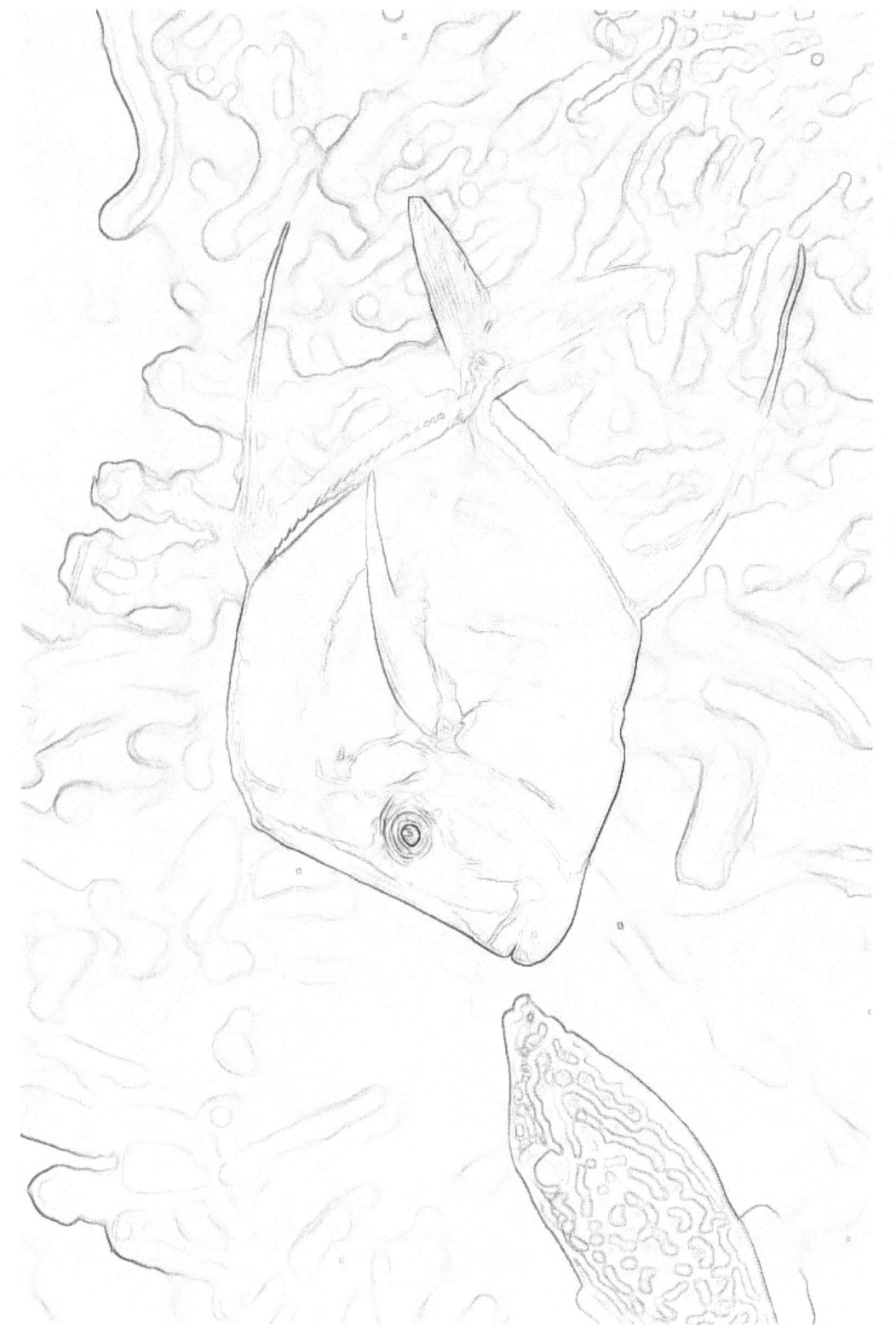

Lookdown (Selene vomer). Marine fish.

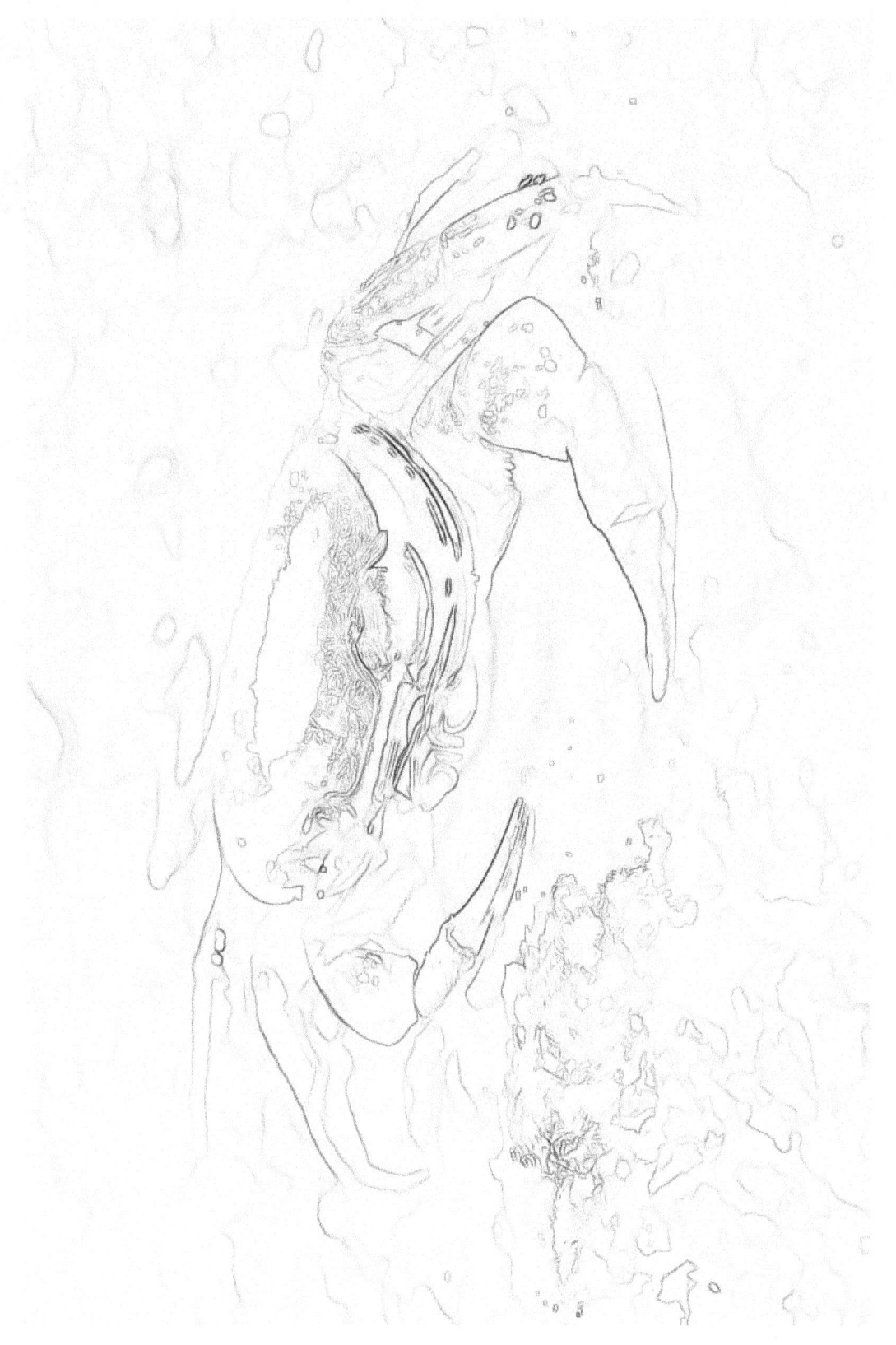

Blackback land crab (Gecarcinus lateralis), also known as the Bermuda land crab

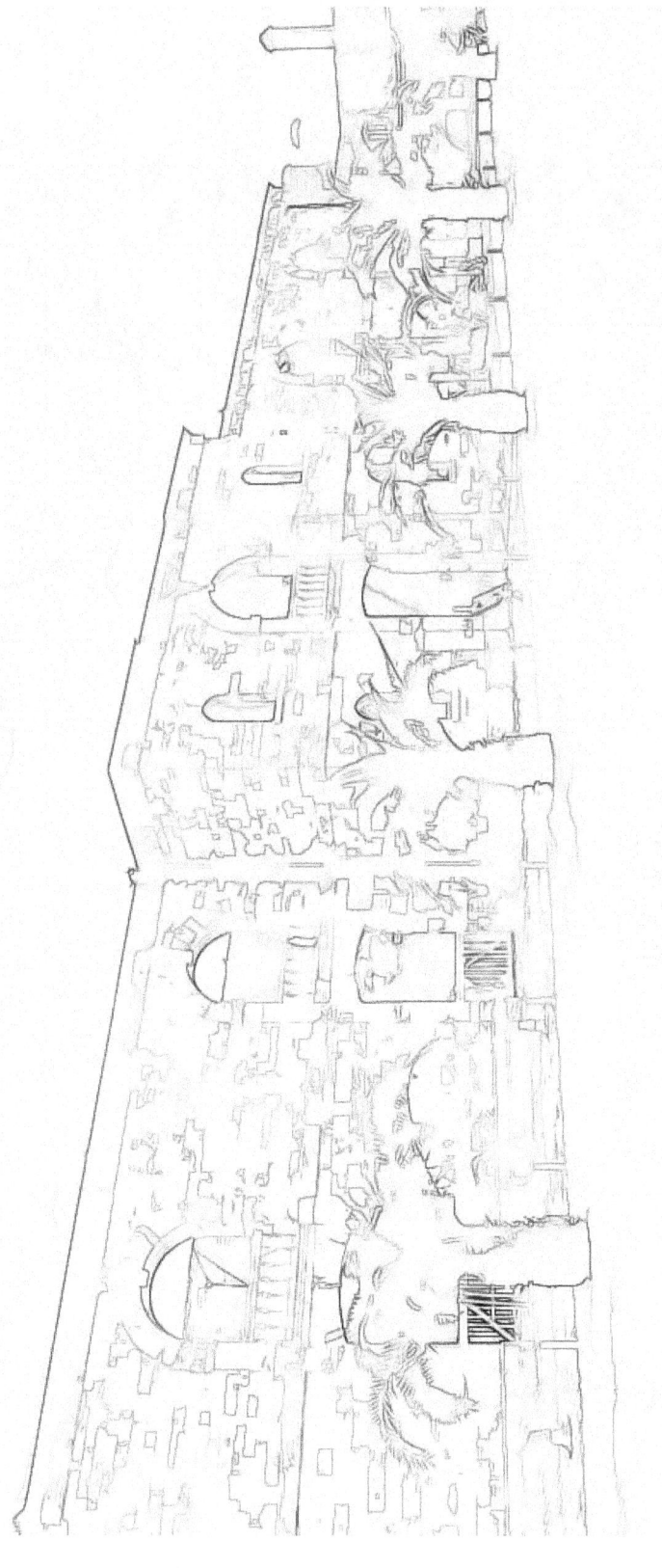

King's Wharf, Bermuda

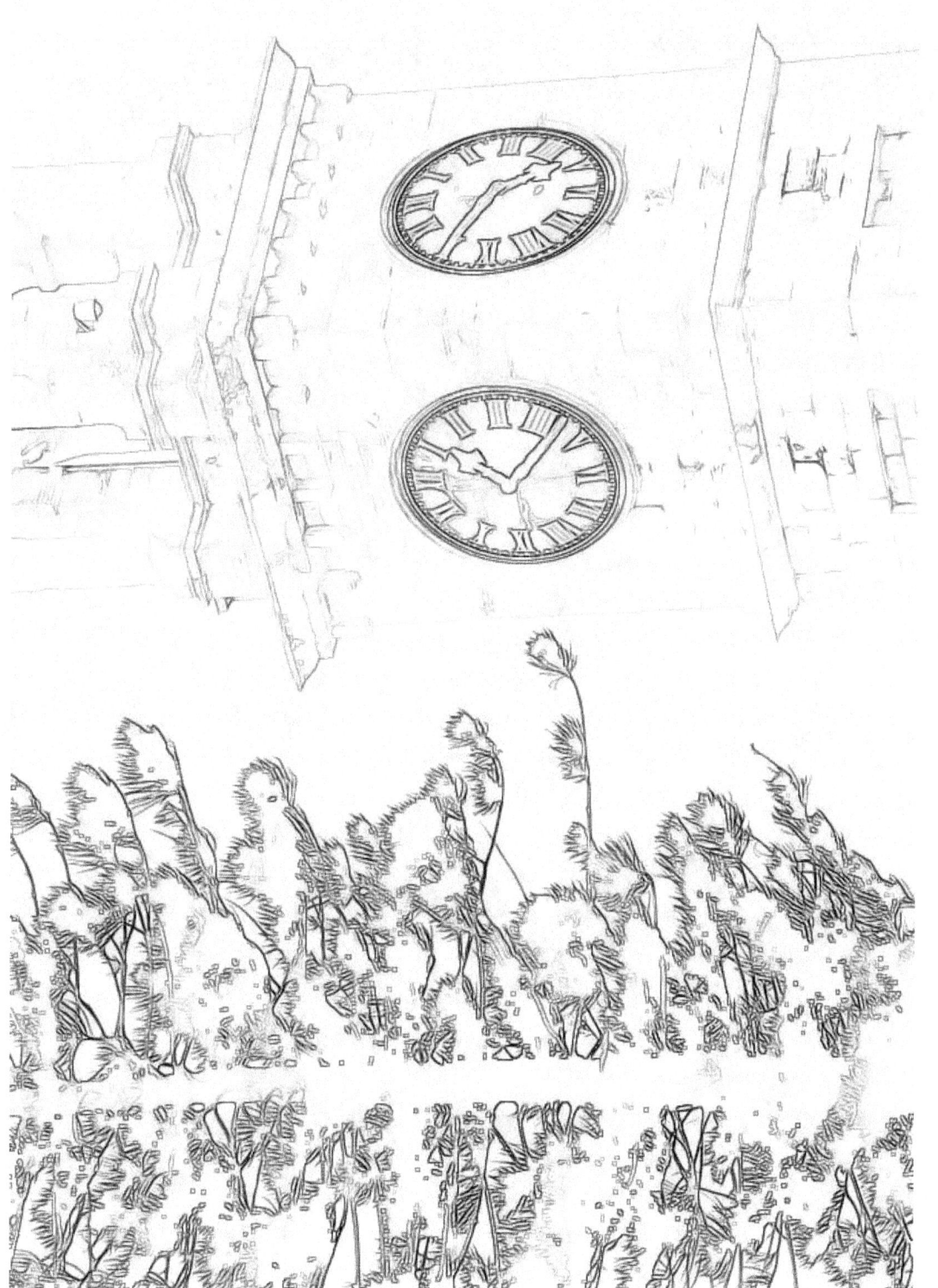

Clock Tower, King's Wharf, Bermuda

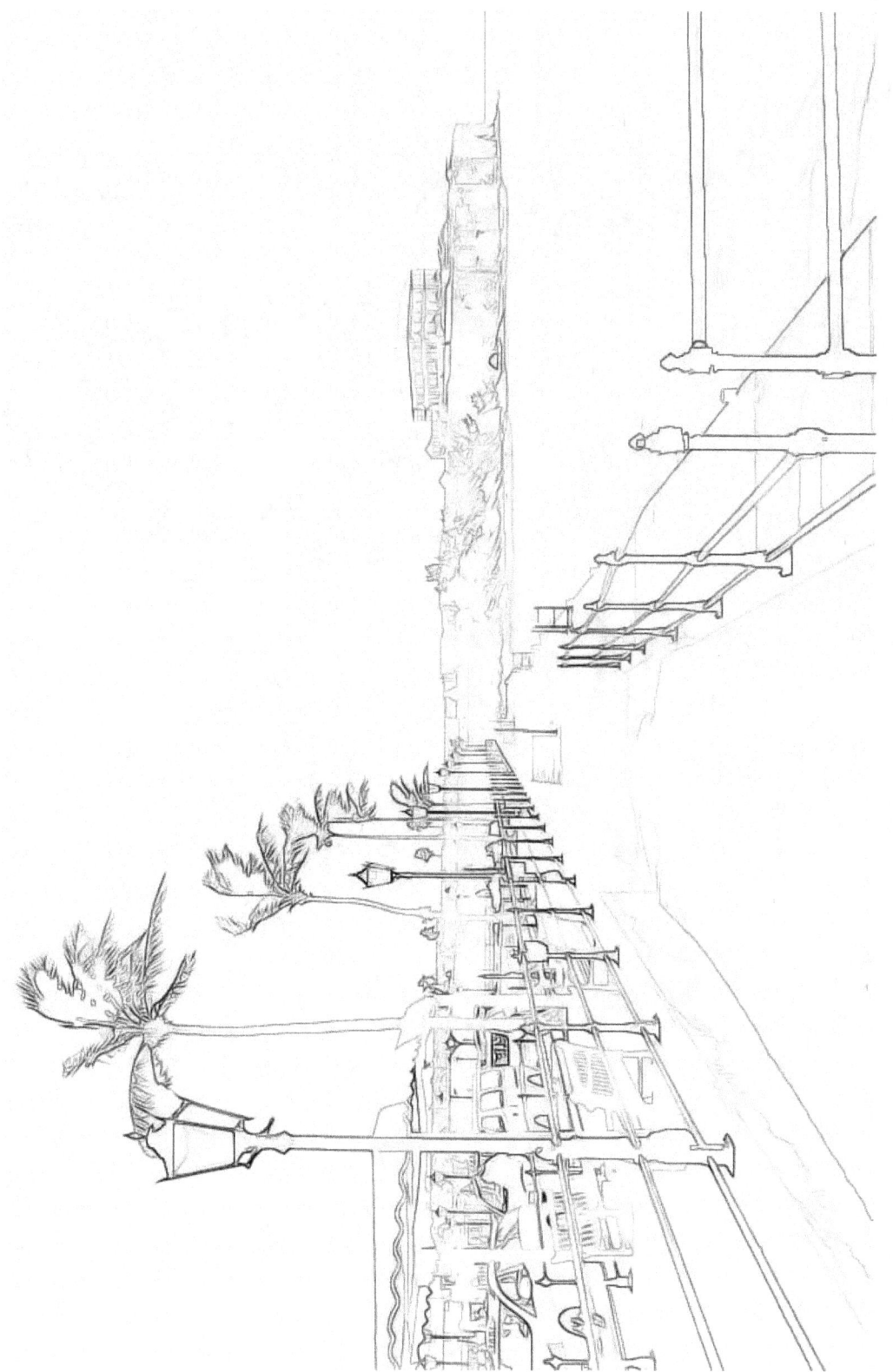

King's Wharf, Bermuda

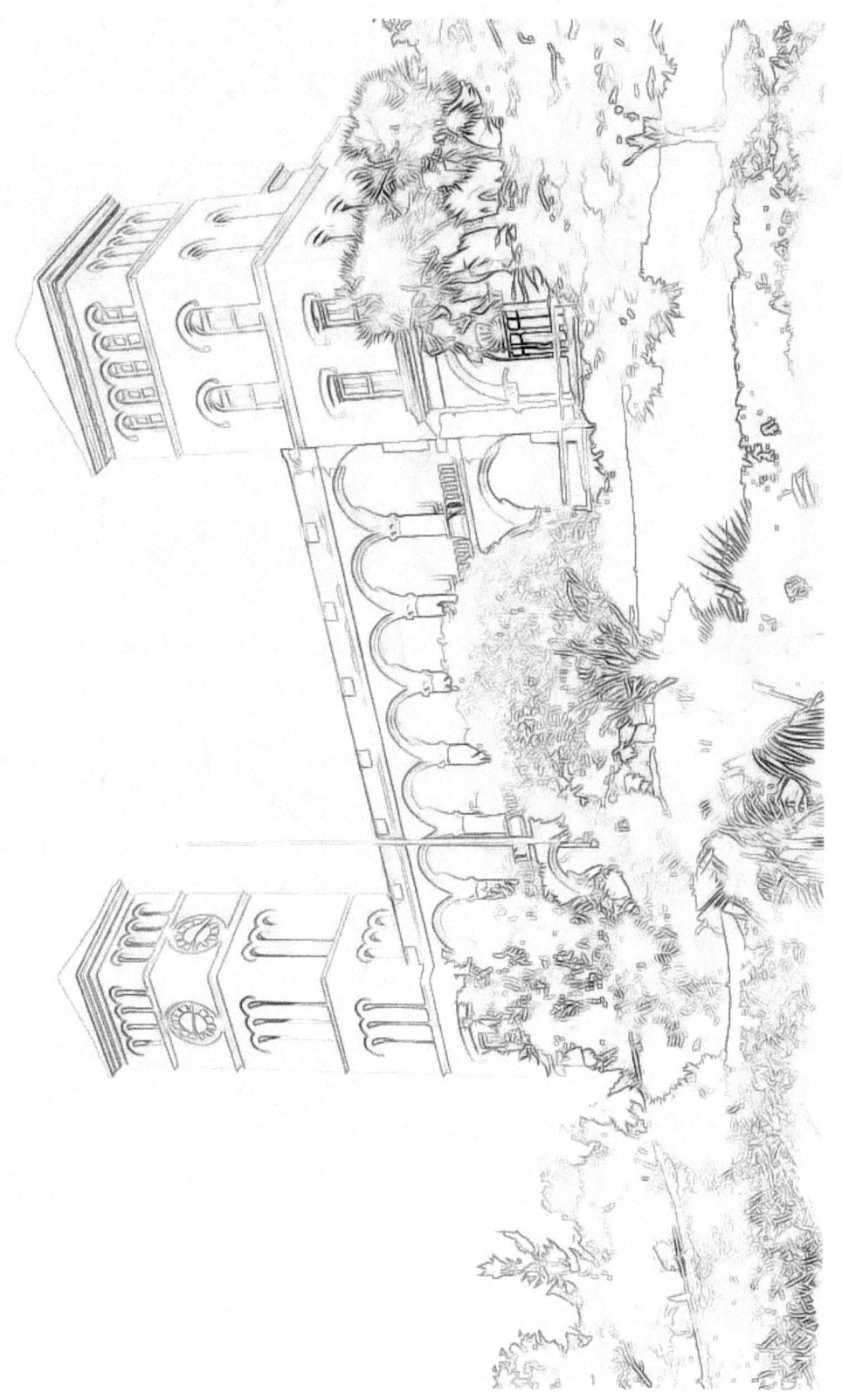

Picture Guide for this book : http://bit.ly/bermuda_best_2017
Don't Miss Another our Books.

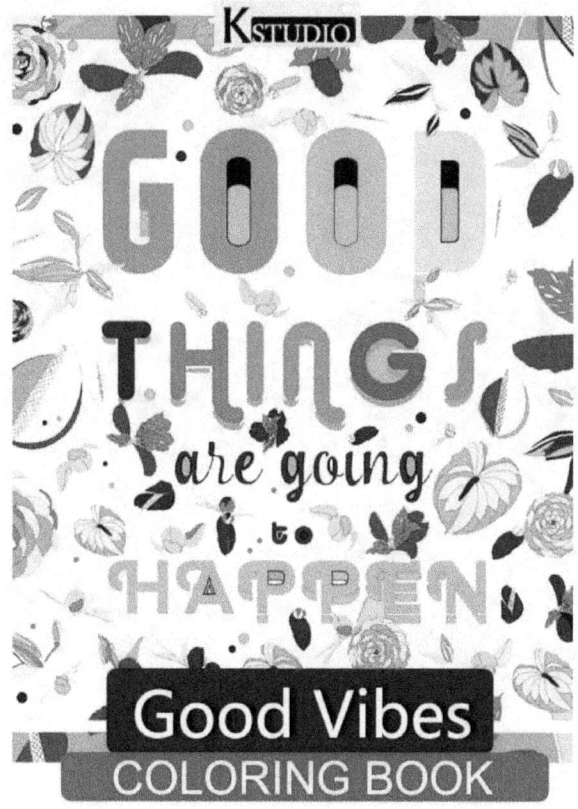

http://bit.ly/good_vibes_1

ISBN : 1530381223
(Use this ISBN for searching on amazon.com)